Bye-Bye
BIDEN

Copyright 2024, Howard G. Peretz

All rights reserved.

No part of this book may be reproduced or shared by any electronic or mechanical means, including but not limited to printing, file sharing, and email, without prior written permission from bestofbiden@gmail.com

ISBN: 978-1-962402-43-9

For more information contact:

peretzhoward@gmail.com

Cover Note: The cover, in a in a whimsical way, shows Harris, dressed as Trump ala Biden's remark, "Look, I wouldn't have picked vice president Trump to be vice president if she was not qualified to be president," giving Biden a backhanded butt slap to hurry him out of office, as Obama, the head puppeteer, looks on from the shadows.

*"I don't make jokes.
I just watch the government and report the facts."*

— Will Rogers,
American entertainer, radio personality, film actor, and writer

Table of Contents

Word Salad #3: *"You think you just fell out of a coconut tree?"* — KH

Word Salad #4: *"…Russia decided to invade a smaller country called Ukraine. So, basically, that's wrong."* — KH

Word Salad #5: *"And I haven't been to Europe. And I mean, I don't understand the point that you're making. I'm not discounting the importance of the border."* — KH

Word Salad #6: *"…What can be, unburdened by what has been…"*— KH

Operation Cover Up

A Note from the Author

President Joe Biden, now 81-years of age, showed early signs of dementia almost from the start of his Presidency. His wife, Dr. Jill, was the lead in trying to keep his\ symptoms secret. This became almost impossible, as America witnessed his decline every time he appeared in public. The evidence continued to pile up as he had multiple slips and falls, including going up the stairs of Air Force 1, word salad statements, forgetting where he was and having to be led by aides, slurring words, and on and on.

Key elements of this cover-up campaign included: lying to the media, extensive use of the teleprompter (Biden even once said the word pause out loud in public) and written note cards, limited press conferences where reporters were given the questions ahead of time and were not allowed to go off script, little transparency on medical records, and extensive down time in Delaware away from the White House. The White House Press Secretary was made the point person on this strategy, as she continued to say, "No one works as hard as he does or can keep up with him — you need to watch him behind closed doors."

If Biden had not insisted on a second term, they would have gotten away with their scheme to deceive the world. He insisted on running again though, and that's when it all fell apart. Even though his debate with Trump included rules intended to help him get through it with minimal issues, in the end there was no way to cover up just how much he had deteriorated.

After the fact, the White House and press said he'd just had a bad night, but we all witnessed it in living color and there was no denying it at this point. As a result, the cover-up pivoted and began to spread the narrative that his original plan was to be a one-term transitional figure and he would step down at the end of his first term.

This presented a problem for the Democratic party because VP Kamala Harris, who initially checked all of the boxes they found desirable — female, youthful, woman of color — did not poll well with the voting public. She, however, is bullet proof because she is the only way they can use the Biden $240 million war chest to fund the campaign. If she isn't the nominee, the party would face refunding money to donors.

It will be interesting to see what happens with those behind the scenes puppeteers who used to direct Biden's every move. What will Dr. Jill, who has been frequently accused of elder care abuse by the opposition; Barack Obama, who was fine with Joe as his two-term vice president but had trouble mitigating Biden's repeated public gaffes while staying in the background; Nancy Pelosi and Chuck Schumer will do now.

Howard G. Peretz
peretz.howard@gmail.com
August 2024

Statistics Don't Lie, But…

Politicians don't seem to understand that just because the inflation rate goes down, it doesn't mean Americans can suddenly afford food and rent.

Zelinski the Super Salesman

Zelinski doesn't mind being called Putin as long as Biden keeps the dollars flowing, he just keeps whispering the magic word into Biden's ear: NATO.

Unsolved White House Cocaine Mystery

Secret Service's "intensive" investigation yields no forensic evidence and with no suspects, so it's now considered a cold case.

Biden's Foreign Policy Blows Whichever Way the Polls Go

Witness Biden's botched withdrawal from Afghanistan, which was seen as one of his greatest strengths by the anti-war left. Because Biden insisted it had to be completed within his first year in office, the outcome was a fiasco and has been called "the Great Humbling."

Biden's Foreign Policy Blows Whichever Way the Polls Go

Judge Brown: 'You Can't Define What a Woman is?'

This leads Americans to wonder how Biden's SCOTUS appointee can hope to vote on reproductive rights.

Judge Brown: 'What Do You Mean, You Can't Define What a Woman is?'

Another Hitch in Biden's Green New Deal Plan

Regarding Biden's plan for EV military vehicles, Matt Pottinger, Deputy National Security Adviser said, "I encountered a lot of IEDs on dirt roads in Afghanistan, but no charging stations." Maybe Biden can't remember what happened in the Battle of the Bulge.

Is there a Doctor in the House? Certainly not in the White House!

In settings or situations where their expertise is not relevant, it's obnoxious and more than a little pretentious for a PhD to insist people refer to them as "doctor."

Is there a Doctor in the House? Certainly not in the White House!

It's Your Debt, Not Ours!

Biden's unconstitutional college loan forgiveness schemes put undue stress on already over-taxed Amercians and do nothing to address the actual problems — high interest on student loans and out of control tuition costs.

It's Your Debt, Not Ours!

Bagel Sales Soar, Keeping Pace with US Rise in Anti-Semitism

US anti-Semitic incidents, including assault, vandalism and harassment, hit record high amid war in Gaza

Trump Doubles Down on Debate

Trump calls for a debate with Harris on his terms, with a "full arena audience," hosted by Fox News after backing out of an ABC News-hosted event that was planned before Biden left the race.

Biden Tries to One-Up Trump in Real Estate Holdings

Jealous of Trump's Mar-a-Lago estate, Biden becomes "The Big Guy" with family money purchasing the resort city of Rehoboth Beach in Delaware, population 1500.

Harris Claims a Number-One Spot

Harris has finally won something — "Best Word Salad Spouting Political Figure." She secured this title after the previous titleholder, Biden, dropped out of the presidential race.

Is There a Printing Press in the Delaware Mansion Basement?

Biden's $7.2 trillion spending spree would certainly indicate he believes there's a printing press in his basement that runs 24/7. Experts are predicting he will have overseen a net increase in US debt during his administration of $9 trillion — a new record. This author wonders just how much Hunter "smartest man" Biden managed to skim off the top, since his art sales have become non-existent.

Biden Siphons SPR, Leaves US Vulnerable

In a bid to gain votes by lowering gas prices before the election, Biden depleted the Strategic Oil Reserve by 45% and has yet to replace it due to high oil prices.

Uneducated Gen Zs Pose Danger to Future Freedom

Woefully uneducated Gen Zers think
the United States is the worst country
around and that its history is heinous,
so they willingly promote socialism
and communism because they've been
indoctrinated and believe those are bettter
than our Constitution.

'Catch and Release' Only for Fishing

Biden's Catch and Release Operation for illegal immigrants has exacerbated the raging crisis at the southern border by releasing over 75% of illegals encountered by Border Patrol into the country illegally.

'Catch and Release' Only for Fishing, Not Illegals

Biden Attempts to Erase Trump Legacy

On day one of his Presidency, Biden worked overtime to erase his predicesor's legacy through copious Executive Orders. Among orders were narrowing the number of unauthorized immigrants vulnerable to arrest, detention and removal; lifting barriers to U.S. entry and to accessing immigration benefits; raising the refugee resettlement ceiling to 125,000; protecting as many as 1 million noncitizens from deportation and giving them eligibility to apply for a work permit.

Abraham Accords Gamble Brings Devastating Consequences

Biden's attempts to turn away from the region were out the window after the Oct. 7, 2023, Hamas assault on Israel, representing a total failure of Biden's Middle East policy.

Bibi Delivers Master Class Without Teleprompter

Israeli Prime Minister Bibi Netanyahu spoke before a joint session of Congress on July 24, 2024, giving a combined a lesson in history and politics as he explained what VP Harris' often quoted "from the river to the sea" chant actually means. Of course, VP Harris wasn't there to be educated — she opted to speak at a small sorority gathering in the red state of Indiana instead.

Shuttle Diplomacy Earns Little Other Than Air Miles

Antony Blinken, an academic who follows
in the tradition of Neville Chamberlain
who believed Hitler wanted peace, believes
his shuttle diplomacy is the way to solve
the Middle East crisis, as in walk softly and
carry a licorice stick
(aka clarinet).

Weaponize the DOJ to Eliminate Those Pesky Political Foes

Biden weaponized the Department of Justice in an attempt to take out political opponent Trump through the justice system with help from former Obama wingman AG Eric Holder and Merrick Garland.

Don't Like the SCOTUS Rulings, Just 'Delegitimize' Them

Biden, who was displeased by recent conservative SCOTUS rulings — especially those favoring rival Trump — proposed ethics code and term limits for justices in an attempt to rein them in.

Science?
We Don't Need No Stinkin' Science

Ignoring scientific understanding of what
is male and female, i.e. chromosome
makeup, of XX for women and XY for men,
Democrat-favored Gender Affirming Care
encourages children to
"self-determine" their gender with no
parental input allowed.

Biden Dems Favor 'Mob Rule'

Merrick Garland and big city prosecutors refuse to make examples of Liberal rioters and other violent protesters and decline to press charges after they destroy public and private property.

Biden Administration SCOTUS Leak Never Solved

After 126 interviews and eight months, the Supreme Court Marshal has failed to find the source of the leaked *Roe v. Wade* opinion draft.

DEI Backlash Spreads to States

Biden Administration DEI proponents are finding it more and more difficult to defend their pet project as states officially oppose DEI policies of equality over equity.

Biden Living the American Dream

Only in America can someone go from
being a government salaried grunt to a
multi-millionaire leader of the free world
who only works from parttime Monday
through Friday with no calls after 4 p.m.
and no weekend hours.

Debate debacle
No Surprise to Anyone

After Biden's debate debacle against Trump, there was no shortage of "I told you so" sentiment circulated by Biden opponents who indicated they'd known about Biden's issues for a "long time."

First Lady Faux Pas

In a case of poor timing, Dr. Jill graces the cover of *Vogue* four days after Sleepy Joe's devastating debate disaster brought fresh scrutiny to her role in covering up her husband's declining health to retain her own political power and prestige.

How Many Gaffes Does It Take to Get to the Center of a Political Cover-up?

Apparently, the number is infinite if you look at Biden's prolific "gaffe machine" and the way the liberal media blatantly ignores everything negative their "golden" boy said and did.

How Many Gaffes Does It Take to Get to the Center of a Political Cover-up?

I Beg Your Pardon…

Will Biden find a way to pardon family members before leaving office, even though Presidents do not have the power to pardon state charges?

I Beg Your Pardon...

Failed "Don't" Doctrine

Biden's "Don't, Don't, Don't" response to the Hamas-led massacre against Israel was unsurprisingly not an effective deterrent against genocidal regimes bent on the destruction of Israel.

Creepy Joe the Whisperer

Even though he has a "whisper coach,"
Biden's use of this ploy falls flat with world
media and helps to further cement
his image on the world stage
as creepy and strange.

Creepy Joe the Whisperer

Commander 24, Secret Service 0

Biden's lack of authority extended even to his dog, who bit more than 24 Secret Service agents before he was finally "banished" from the White House.

'Joe Cool' He is Not

Biden, regardless of his fondness for Aviator shades, vintage Corvettes, double scoops of Graeter's chocolate chip ice cream, and screaming from the rooftops about student loan relief just doesn't have the power to sway younger voters who see him as too old and out of touch to understand their needs.

'Free Speech too Unfettered' says Biden Team Leader

Biden's people want to redefine freedom of speech to make "hate" speech a crime, saying all speech is not equal and current thoughts on freedom of speech are outdated.

American Dream Canceled

Bidenonomics forced America into a new era of super government control, reckless government spending, unprecedented national debt and out of control inflation that has made the American dream unreachable for most.

Dems Prone to Eating Their Own

Press Secretary Karine Jean-Pierre learned this the hard way when she was nearly ousted by her own party, which used a cloak-and-dagger scheme intended to pressure her to step down.

Obama, Secret Cabaal: Master Puppeteers?

Opponents claim Biden wasn't capable of making decisions on his own during his Presidential term, and was totally controlled by people in the shadows.

Too Little, Too Late

Biden's border policies and resulting mismanagement by his VP turned Presidential nominee earned him the lowest approval rating ever, so in an attempt to recover in the polls he finally imposed restrictions in June 2024.

Biden Administration Stomps Women's Rights

Biden's efforts to appease the Alphabet Community have subverted Title IX and used it to sacrifice biological females on the trans-equality altar by allowing biological male transgender athletes to complete against biological females with dream-shattering and often dangerous results.

#Gotaways Trending

In less than four years, more than 1.7 million "gotaways" have made their way over the southern border without apprehension due to Biden's lax border policies — this number is more than the combined total recorded from 2010-2020.

Taxpayers Stuck Paying as Illegals Basically Dine and Dash

American taxpayers are footing the $400 billion cost of Biden's open border policies, with the lion's share of that borne by state and local governments — meaning higher taxes and fewer services for actual citizens.

Taxpayers Stuck Paying as Illegals Dine and Dash

China Biggest Threat — Just Ask Taiwan

Biden's worry about global warming and farting cows pales in comparison to the actual threat from China, which is also one of the biggest CO_2 and other toxic pollution offenders in the world.

Same Offense, Different Consequences

Apparently, a failing memory earns pity and a pass from prosecutors for Biden's classified document stash, while Trump faces criminal charges for the exact same offense.

In 2020 Peaceful Protests = Riots

More than 10,000 were arrested in the wake
of George Floyd's death, with many charged
with burglary, looting, assaults on police
and other violence as they
"peacfully" protested.
What compounded the outrage over these
actions was nearly all of those arrested were
ultimately released without being charged.

In 2020 Peaceful Protests = Riots

January 6 Protest Deemed 'Insurrection' for Political Gain

The amount of time, energy and money spent leveling charges against participants and prosecuting something that was essentially a non-event has cost American taxpayers at minimum $36 million — and it isn't over.

The Laptop from Hell

Sources say CIA officials at the highest level colluded with the Biden Campaign to discredit the Hunter Biden laptop story just weeks before the 2020 Presidential election, promoting a narrative of foreign election interference instead.

Erasing History
One Monument at a Time

Uneducated, misguided individuals seem to feel that desecrating or even removing historic landmarks will somehow erase history they do not want to acknowledge exists, and the Biden Administration seems happy to go along with this thinking.

'Dazed and Confused' Means You Lose

Biden's disastrous 2024 debate against Donald Trump sealed his fate with staff, supporters and most importantly big dollar donors, who all recommended he step down due to his age and visible cognitive decline.

Cognition Hoax

Many have alleged that senior Democrats conspired to hide the truth about the President's health from the American public and allowed unnamed staffers to run the country in his place since he took office in 2020.

Democrat Sharks Smell Blood

Nancy Pelosi and other high-ranking Democrats had no qualms about jumping ship once it became clear Biden's issues could no longer be covered up.

'Woke' Hiring Practices Backfire

After the Secret Service's failure to detect
and take out the sniper who attempted
to assassinate former President Trump,
Director Cheatle's DEI hiring practices have
called into question the quality and training
of agents hired under her watch.

Ridiculous Rushmore Recommendation

In an effort to convince the to smooth Biden's ruffled feathers after she led efforts to remove him from the Presidential ticket, former House Speaker Nancy Pelosi mused that Biden should be added to Mount Rushmore, saying he was, "Such a consequential president of the United States, a Mount Rushmore kind of president..."

Ridiculous Rushmore Suggestion

Divine Intervention or Ron Johnson?

The investigation into the attempted Trump assassination has highlighted Secret Service ineptness and agency scrambling to deflect blame, including FBI Director Christopher Wray who said, "There's some question about whether or not it's a bullet or shrapnel" that hit the former president. In reality Wisconsin Senator Ron Johnson is the real hero, since he provided the chart Trump turned to look at while addressing the crowd at the Butler Farm Show grounds, foiling the assassination attempt.

Divine Intervention or Ron Johnson?

Last Grasp for Power

Biden is making a last-ditch effort to clap back at political rivals by "reforming" the Supreme Court, including pushing for a "No One is Above the Law Amendment," and attempting to neuter the SCOTUS through term limits and a binding code of conduct.

Out with a Whimper Not a Bang

Biden ended his re-election bid with an
unofficial Tweet on X and similar posts
on other social media that surprised even
senior campaign and White House officials.

Everybody Hates Me, Guess I'll Go Eat Worms…

After it became clear that *absolutely no one* wanted him to continue his re-election bid, Biden reluctantly endorsed VP Harris to take his place.

The Queen of Flip-Flops

VP turned Democratic Presidential nominee Kamala Harris has already repeatedly proved she's the best at going whichever way the wind blows as she flip-flops her stance on major issues just days after becoming the Presidential nominee.

VPs Just 'Do The Dew'

The anticipated VP debate between Progressive Tim Walz and Trump loyalist JD Vance will likely be a dud as both participants agreed after media scrutiny their favorite beverage Diet Mt. Dew.

Prosecutor vs. Felon

Will this be the Progressive Left's title for the
first Harris and Trump debate?

The Rest of the Story...

The following pages are dedicated to
Joe Biden's many other accomplishments
while in office.

The Rest of the Story...

My Kind of Candidate

Will Rodgers (1879-1935), known as the "Cowboy Philosopher," was an actor, humorous and political philosopher the most beloved American in the 1920s. His earthy anecdotes and folksy style allowed him to poke fun at everyone from gangsters to prohibition, politicians, and a host of other controversial topics in a way that was appreciated by a national audience, with no one offended.

One of his widely quoted comments was, "I am not a member of an organized political party. I am a Democrat."

In May 1928, *Life* magazine ran an entertaining story promoting the idea that Will Rogers was running for President of the United States. The article appealed to "dissatisfied voters of both parties," saying Rogers was a perfect fit for the candidacy. Rogers penned a witty retort the following week with the headline: I Accept the Nomination. He continued by saying the platform of his candidacy would be: "Whatever the other fellow don't do, we will."

Rogers thought all political campaigning was bunk, so to prove that point he ran as the "bunkless candidate" of the Anti-Bunk Party. His only campaign promise was that, if elected, he would resign.

Every week, from Memorial Day through Election Day, Rogers caricatured the farcical humors of grave campaign politics. Then, on election day he declared victory and promptly resigned.

www.ingramcontent.com/pod-product-compliance
Lightning Source LLC
Chambersburg PA
CBHW071328120626
46546CB00002B/484